LEADERS OF
ANCIENT GREECE

LEONIDAS Hero of
Thermopylae

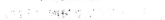

LEADERS OF ANCIENT GREECE

LEONIDAS

Hero of Thermopylae

Ian Macgregor Morris

the rosen publishing center's
rosen
central

Published in 2004 by The Rosen Publishing Group, Inc.
29 East 21st Street, New York, NY 10010

First Edition

Library of Congress Cataloging-in-Publication Data

Morris, Ian Macgregor.
Leonidas: hero of Thermopylae / Ian Macgregor Morris.
    p. cm. — (Leaders of ancient Greece)
Includes bibliographical references and index.
ISBN 0-8239-3827-1
1. Leonidas, King of Sparta, d. 480 B.C. 2. Sparta (Extinct
city)—History. 3. Thermopylae, Battle of, 480 B.C.
4. Sparta (Extinct city)—Kings and rulers—Biography.
I. Title. II. Series.
DF226.L46 M67 2003
938'.903'092—dc21

                                        2002006688

Manufactured in the United States of America

CONTENTS

In life, since all men must die, since death is inevitable, why would any man choose to grow old and bitter in the darkness, avoiding glory and honor?

—Pindar, fifth century BC

I came to myself in a great stillness, to realize I was standing by the little mound. This is the mound of Leonidas, with its dust and rank grass, its flowers and lizards, its stones, scruffy laurels, and hot gusts of wind. I knew now that something real happened here.

—William Golding,
The Hot Gates, 1965

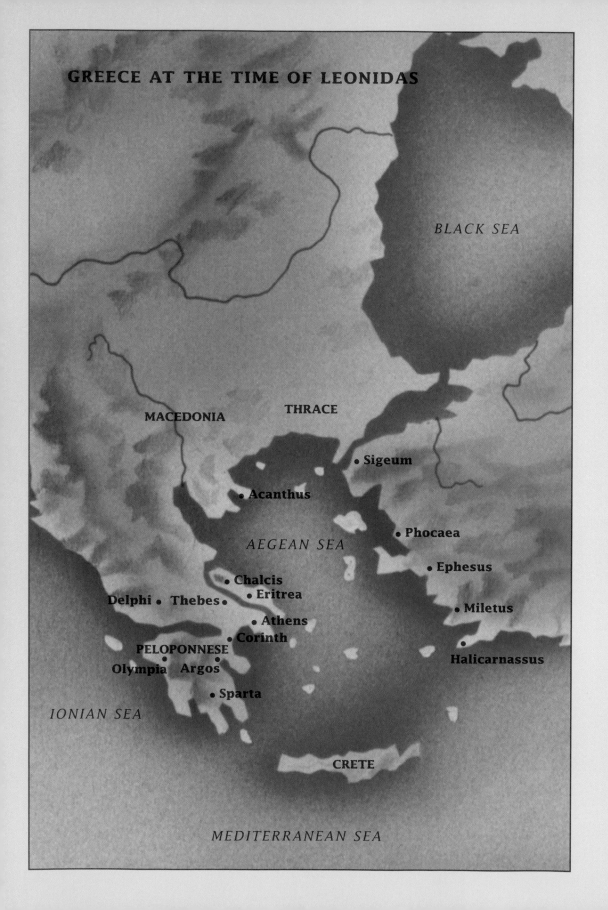

GREECE AT THE TIME OF LEONIDAS

BLACK SEA

MACEDONIA   THRACE

• Sigeum

• Acanthus

AEGEAN SEA

• Phocaea

• Ephesus

• Chalcis
Delphi •   Thebes •   • Eritrea

• Miletus

• Athens
• Corinth

PELOPONNESE

Olympia •   • Argos

• Halicarnassus

• Sparta

IONIAN SEA

CRETE

MEDITERRANEAN SEA

INTRODUCTION

The story of Leonidas is a remarkable one. Born in the sixth century BC, he became the king of Sparta, one of the most powerful states in the Mediterranean. However, we know comparatively little about his life. It was his death that made him a legend.

During the fifth century BC, when Leonidas was king of Sparta, the Greek people had no concept of nation or nationality. They lived in small separate cities, each fiercely independent. Although they shared a language and worshiped the same gods, there was no unity or sense of obligation between them. Each Greek lived and died within and for his or her city. Most Greeks would much rather have allied themselves with a foreign power than with a neighboring Greek city, called a *polis* (plural *poleis*). Although "polis"

A fifth-century-BC bust thought to represent King Leonidas of Sparta

is usually translated as "city-state," this conveys only part of the meaning. English words such as "politics" and "politicians" are derived from this term, and that is no coincidence. To the Greeks, the ideal life was the political life. The philosopher Aristotle claimed that man is a "political animal," a "creature of the polis." The state was the body of citizens themselves and guaranteed the rights of the citizens. The Greeks viewed other forms of government, such as the great monarchies in Asia, as forms of tyranny in which people were not free.

The polis was usually small. If all the citizens were to participate directly in the government, there could not be too many of them. A large number of citizens would mean the voice of the individual was insignificant. A large polis, such as Athens, had less than 30,000 citizens; but most had only a few hundred. There were a huge number of independent poleis, up to five or six hundred at any one time. This gave the individuals within each polis a considerable amount of freedom and influence in the running of their city. However, the citizens of the poleis viewed one another with suspicion, so that when a powerful enemy threatened there was little hope of a defensive alliance. Indeed, when the Persians invaded Greece in 480 BC, many of the Greek poleis actually joined the Persian side. The price of such freedom was great instability.

Each polis had its own form of government or constitution. Some were radically democratic; others were forms of monarchy. However, most had very complex systems of government, and none was more complex than that of Sparta. Before the story of Leonidas can be told, we must briefly consider the city in which he lived, and what made it unique.

Sparta was situated in southern Greece, in an area known as the Peloponnese. The city lay between two mountain ranges in a lush valley that opened to the sea. However, the Spartans

Between these mountainous crags lies the site of the ancient city-state of Sparta.

controlled land far beyond the valley. By the time of Leonidas, the Spartans were the most powerful people in all of Greece. Part of their power lay in the fact that, unlike any other Greek city, the Spartans had a permanent standing army. In other cities, when danger threatened, the citizens would leave their normal occupations, gather their weapons, and march out to face the enemy. The Spartans, however, were professional soldiers, and rather than work at ordinary tasks they spent most of their time in military training. They were able to do this because they controlled a large slave population called *helots*. Every Greek city had a large slave population, but the slaves in Sparta were essential to the city's welfare. The helots were descended from the conquered populations of the areas of Laconia and Messenia in southern Greece. They were the laborers of Sparta. While the citizen class trained for war, the helots farmed the land and

A sixth-century-BC statue of a Spartan warrior armed for battle and wearing his military cloak

provided the food that made the Spartans' lifestyle possible. Much like serfs during the Middle Ages, helots were forced to give a fixed amount of all the food they produced to their Spartan masters. However, unlike most of the slaves in Greece, they lived in communities and had their own families. On occasion they also served the Spartan warriors on campaign.

The helot population outnumbered the Spartans by as much as three to one, and the threat of a slave revolt continually worried the Spartan authorities. Indeed, this fear often dictated Spartan foreign policy. Because of the helots, the Spartans never wanted to send their army too far away from Sparta. The great irony is that while the helots allowed the Spartans to have a permanent standing army, at the same time the threat of helot revolt made such an army necessary. The Spartans tried to keep the helots under strict control. There are many examples of brutal treatment of the helots by the Spartans. The Crypteia, a secret police force, was formed to watch the helots. Despite this treatment, however, the helots rarely revolted and often served loyally next to their Spartan masters in battle.

This urn shows Helots harvesting grapes. In Sparta, the land was worked by the helots, or slaves, freeing the Spartans for military service.

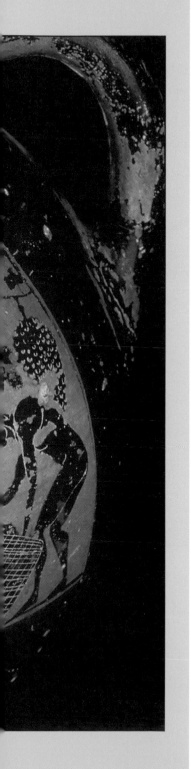

While the helots carried out the menial work in Sparta, members of the middle class carried out the more technical tasks. These people were called the *perioeci*. They were not full citizens, but unlike the helots they had some legal rights. The perioeci lived in their own towns and controlled their own internal affairs, but paid taxes to the Spartan government and served in the Spartan army. They were the industrial workforce of the Spartan state and carried out the commercial and manufacturing work that had to be done.

With the helots and perioeci under their control, the Spartan citizens were free from the day-to-day tasks that the poorer citizens of other cities often had to do for themselves. Within this citizen class, the Spartans believed in a strict equality, so that even the kings possessed only minor privileges. According to tradition, this equality was achieved by a remarkable political system devised by Lycurgus, a Spartan statesman, in the eighth century BC. The system ensured that no one person could dominate and that Sparta would remain stable and free from the civil strife that plagued most Greek cities. Sparta was ruled jointly by two kings. There are various legends surrounding this arrangement, but historians believe that the dual kingship in Sparta was the result of the unification of several villages and that the leaders of these communities decided to share power.

After the reforms of Lycurgus, the power of the kings was severely limited. Unlike the all-powerful kings of Persia, the kings of Sparta were subject to the law like any other citizen. The only time a king had undisputed power was while he was in command of the army. The king could be deposed at any time and could be put on trial, exiled, or even executed. To be a Spartan king was not just an honor; it was a duty, an act of service to the people. In fact, the kings of Sparta were the very first constitutional monarchs.

Lycurgus created a council of elders, a public assembly, and special magistrates called ephors. The council of elders, or *gerousia* (from the ancient Greek "gerontes," meaning "old men"), consisted of the two kings and twenty-eight men over the age of sixty. Only men from certain aristocratic families were eligible; they were elected in a very unusual way. Each of the candidates for election would be brought before the public assembly in turn, and the people would cheer for the one they wished to see elected. A panel of judges, who could not see the candidates, sat behind a wall. The judges would listen to the cheering of the crowd and note the candidate who received the greatest acclaim. Once elected, the members of the council would hold their position for life. It was their duty to prepare business for the assembly and to act as judges in serious court cases.

The public assembly was open to all male citizens over the age of thirty. It was their duty to elect the members of the gerousia and the ephors. The assembly had the power to declare war and to approve peace treaties, as well as to appoint army commanders. The assembly accepted or rejected laws proposed by the gerousia. However, they could not propose laws or debate them, like the citizens of Athens. Without the agreement of the people, Sparta could not declare war; this is often seen as a key part of the freedom the ancient Greeks enjoyed.

Five ephors were elected every year in the same manner as the members of the gerousia. It was their duty to oversee meetings of the gerousia and the assembly, propose laws, and bring serious legal cases to court, including any prosecution against the king. Indeed, the ephors were the real power in the Spartan state.

In theory, the Spartan constitution formed a perfect balance. To its admirers, each branch of the Spartan government was held in check by the other two branches. The king could not become a tyrant because he was held in check by the power of the ephors and the assembly. The aristocrats in the gerousia could not rule in their own interest because they too needed the support of the people. And the people in the public assembly could not resort to mob rule because the king and gerousia limited the power of the assembly. Although the ephors were very powerful, they could hold their positions for only one year and could not be re-elected. Historians believe that this is the reason that the Spartan state enjoyed such stability for such a long time. During the eighteenth century AD philosophers and politicians who were searching for an alternative to the absolute monarchies of Europe turned to the

A painting of Chilon, who was one of the wise men that served on the council of elders created by Lycurgus

Spartan system as an ideal. The principle of power, limited by the law, provided the inspiration for the leaders of the American and French Revolutions.

Lycurgus's reforms went well beyond the political system. If the citizens were to be truly equal, then all the causes of inequality had to be removed. Of these, the most dangerous was wealth—wealth divides society. The rich, many philosophers have warned, care only for their own wealth, while the poor are jealous of them and seek to become rich themselves. The conflict between rich and poor was a problem in many Greek cities. According to tradition, Lycurgus solved the problem by banning money. Gold and silver were outlawed from the city. Each citizen was given an equal share of land, which was farmed by helots. The citizens were taught to despise wealth as degenerate. Fine foods and material possessions were thought to corrupt people because a higher value was placed on the comforts and luxuries of life than on virtue and honor. The leaders believed that the good life could only be achieved by shunning the pursuit of wealth and serving the community. Thus the Spartans learned to live with a bare minimum of comforts. These principles were taught to young Spartans, including Leonidas. It is from this austere lifestyle that modern English derives the word "spartan," meaning sparse or basic.

Of all the figures in Spartan history, none has been so admired as Leonidas. He came to represent all that was good about Sparta, and indeed ancient Greece. People throughout the ages have imagined Leonidas as their ideal hero. For centuries people have turned to the writings of the historian Herodotus for the story of Leonidas. Herodotus was born just a few years before Leonidas died and had the opportunity to talk to people who had known the Spartan king. The exploits of Leonidas are recorded in Herodotus's history of the great war between Greece and Persia. It is through these writings that we learn of Leonidas. Although later writers add some important details, they must be treated with suspicion. The writer and philosopher Plutarch, and the historian Diodorus of Sicily, wrote their histories several hundred years after Leonidas lived; the stories and traditions they recorded are often viewed as fiction. However, the details that Plutarch and Diodorus include reflect the esteem in which Leonidas was held, and as such have become part of the legend. For the story of Leonidas is not just the story of a man. It is the story of a hero whose fame stretched far beyond Sparta and became part of history itself.

THE CITIZEN

Leonidas was born sometime around the year 535 BC, and was the third son of King Anaxandridas. The events surrounding Leonidas's birth involved a political crisis that would affect his succession to the throne some forty years later.

Anaxandridas had been king for nearly twenty years, but had not fathered a son. The ephors, the annually elected magistrates whose powers surpassed those of the king's, saw a great danger in this. Anaxandridas could trace his lineage back to Eurysthenes, one of the mythical founders of Sparta. If Anaxandridas failed to produce an heir, not only would there be no successor, but the line of Eurysthenes would die out. The Spartans were a superstitious people and proud of their traditions. If one of the royal houses died out, it would be seen as a bad omen for the city; this could not be allowed to happen. So the ephors told Anaxandridas that he must divorce his wife, whom they believed was barren, and take a new wife who could conceive a son. Anaxandridas, however, was very fond of his wife and refused. He believed that she had done nothing wrong and did not deserve the shame and dishonor that divorce would bring. Faced with such a problem, the ephors realized that they had to compromise. They suggested that Anaxandridas could keep his first wife on one condition: Anaxandridas would take a second wife to provide an heir. Anaxandridas knew that to refuse would show disloyalty to the city because he would be placing his own desires above that of the state. So he agreed to this arrangement and took a second wife. He then had two households and two families, something unheard of in Sparta.

Soon after the marriage, Anaxandridas's new wife gave birth to a boy who was named Cleomenes. With his duty done, Anaxandridas turned his attention to his first wife. However, soon after the birth of Cleomenes, his first wife also became pregnant. On hearing this news, the relatives of Anaxandridas's second wife became suspicious. They believed that the first wife, fearing the embarrassment of not being able to produce an heir and jealous of the second wife, was only pretending to be pregnant. When the time came for the child to be born, they claimed, she would find another baby, probably that of a slave, and pass it off as her own. These relatives feared that such a child would have a claim to the throne over that of Cleomenes.

Anaxandridas and his first wife denied these accusations, but the ephors did not know whom to believe. The ephors decided that when the child was due, they would witness the birth. When the time came, the ephors and the members of the council of elders, some thirty-five men in all, gathered to watch. Sure enough, Anaxandridas's first wife gave birth to a healthy baby boy, who was named Dorieus. Soon after, she became pregnant a second time and gave birth to Leonidas. Soon after that she gave birth to a third son, who was named Cleombrotus.

The sons of Anaxandridas by his first wife felt that they had a better claim to the throne than their elder half-brother Cleomenes. They believed that their father had been forced into his second marriage against his will and that such a marriage was a break with Spartan tradition. For his part, Cleomenes could respond that however untraditional the arrangement, it was still legal. Cleomenes was the eldest son of

A relief carving of a Spartan couple from their sarcophagus

the king. Thus was born a rivalry between Cleomenes and Dorieus, each believing that by rights he should be the heir. The rivalry was compounded by their difference in character. Dorieus was known as the finest young man of his generation, possessing all the virtues a Spartan should have. Cleomenes was unstable and prone to fits of madness. However, the legal view of the succession was clear. Cleomenes was the eldest son, and as such he would succeed his father as king of Sparta. The brothers Dorieus, Leonidas, and Cleombrotus would become ordinary Spartan citizens. And as citizens, they had to undergo the brutal Spartan system of education known as the *agoge*.

Sparta possessed an educational system that was unique in both the ancient and modern worlds. At the age of seven, boys left home to enter the agoge, a system of training and education that lasted until they were eighteen. On

A relief carving of two wrestlers

the simplest level, the agoge system sought to turn boys into elite soldiers, disciplined and loyal. However, the system was also designed to produce excellent citizens. For the ancient Greeks, being a soldier was very much part of the duty of a citizen. When the polis was threatened, the citizens gathered to defend it.

It was in the agoge that citizens were taught to shun wealth and luxury. From their arrival, the boys were divided into groups and slept in dormitories. They underwent a harsh routine of physical exercise and training to be obedient. Spartan boys were taught to walk with their hands folded beneath their cloaks and their eyes turned toward the ground, in an act of humility. Adults had the right to discipline any boy they saw misbehaving. At the age of twelve, the boys entered the second stage of their education. The training became more harsh; simple physical exercise was replaced by tests of endurance and skill. The boys were allowed only one piece of clothing, a cloak made of rough linen. They slept on mattresses made from rushes, an uncomfortable bedding at best. Throughout these years, they were given little food; their diet consisted mainly of a porridge-like broth. The boys were expected to steal food to supplement their meager diets, but if caught, they were beaten. This was not meant to encourage criminality, rather to teach them that an army marches on its stomach. The Spartans encouraged their young men to live off the land, to find roots and berries in the forest, or to steal chickens from a farm. This kind of cunning would serve them well in times of war.

Sports played an important role in the agoge. Wrestling was popular throughout Greece, and the Spartans added a number of team sports. They played a ball game that was similar to rugby or football. In another game, two teams tried to push each other into the river. Players were allowed to use almost any

Greek warriors fight over the body of a fallen comrade, a depiction of a scene from the Trojan War

method to defeat their opponents, and serious injuries were common. Yet the teachers helped to foster a sense of team spirit that would prove invaluable in battle.

The Spartan educational system was not entirely physical. Athenian writers used to joke that the Spartans were illiterate and uneducated. However, the Athenians were sworn enemies of the Spartans for most of the classical period (479–323 BC), and insulted them whenever they could. Even though the Spartans did not possess a rich literary and theatrical culture like Athens, they still had their own arts. The Spartan poets Tyrtaeus and Alcman, who lived during the seventh century BC, were highly respected; their poems were sung at festivals. Singing and dancing played an important part in the education of the boys. At religious festivals, choirs from different age groups would compete against one another. Songs and dances taught

A painting of a Spartan mother with a child in a high chair. In Athens, infants were wrapped in swaddling clothes. In Sparta, this was not done, presumably to toughen up the children.

the boys to work together so that in battle they would be used to working as a single unit. Reading and writing were also important.

During these years, the boys would be under the charge of an *eiren*, a nineteen-year-old who had just completed his own education. Once they reached this age, they too could expect to be put in charge of their own company of boys. As young men, the students were not yet considered fully trained soldiers or citizens. They had to wait until they were thirty before they could attend the public assembly. However, between the ages of twenty and thirty, they could be called to serve in the army. Each young man had to be elected to a *syssitia*, a mess hall in which he lived and ate. This was the focus of his daily life for the ten years.

Although the agoge system was a harsh training for boys, it cannot be denied that it produced the best soldiers in all of Greece, as well as citizens who were respected for their virtue. It was the ultimate leveler. The sons of every citizen had to complete the training if they wished to become citizens themselves. The only boy exempt from the system was the heir to the throne. Thus, Leonidas, Dorieus, and Cleombrotus had to undergo this training, while Cleomenes stayed at home with his father. It was this system that produced the Spartan idea of the equals, or *homoioi*. All the citizens in Sparta considered themselves to be equal before the law. All could stand for election to the *ephorate* and attend the public assembly that decided Spartan policy and voted on matters such as war and peace. The Spartans were the first society in Greece to declare that all citizens were equal.

In 520 BC Anaxandridas died. Despite the protests of Dorieus, Cleomenes was made king. At first Dorieus seems to have tolerated this situation, but after a few years he could no longer

A painting of a laundress at work

live under his half-brother's rule. So he decided to leave Sparta and to found a new city with his followers. This was not unusual in other Greek cities, but very rare at Sparta. Moreover, Dorieus left, in the words of Herodotus, "in a fit of temper" and neglected to complete the usual formalities for such a mission, the most important of which was to consult the oracle at Delphi. He sailed to Africa, where he founded a new city. Dorieus and his followers prospered for two years but were driven out by the local people living in the area. Returning to Sparta, he decided to set out again and found a city in Sicily. According to tradition, certain areas of Sicily belonged to the descendants of the Greek hero Hercules, who had conquered these lands long before, and so Dorieus concluded that he had the right to settle on this land. Believing that his first expedition failed because he did not consult the gods, he went to the oracle at Delphi, where he was told that he would permanently occupy this land. Eventually Dorieus and his followers reached Sicily, but before they could establish a new city, an army of Sicilians and Phoenicians attacked, killing most of the expedition's members. Ironically, the prophecy of the oracle had been fulfilled: Dorieus did occupy the land permanently, in his grave.

A bronze relief carving of warriors and a chariot. After about 700 BC, the Greeks did not use chariots in war, but only for ceremonial and athletic purposes.

Thus died the man who might have been king. Back in Sparta, one can only imagine the impact this news had on the young Leonidas. His brother had died far from home, driven out by Cleomenes, the man who had taken the throne. If there had been any doubt about their rivalry, it was now confirmed. Moreover, until Cleomenes had a son, Leonidas was first in line to the throne.

THE KING

Cleomenes was king of Sparta for thirty years. In that time he pursued an aggressive foreign policy aimed at strengthening Sparta's position. However, his power was limited by the Spartan constitution. He had to gain the support of the citizens, and his influence was always checked by the gerousia and the ephors. Always on the minds of the members of the councils was the problem of the helots, the slaves who worked the fields that provided the Spartans with their food. The fear of helot revolt determined Spartan policy.

In 499 BC Aristagoras, an ambassador from the city of Miletus, came to Sparta. Although the people in the cities along the coast of Asia Minor, known as Ionia, were Greek, they had been under the control of the mighty Persian Empire for fifty years. Cleomenes was shrewd enough to realize that the Persian Empire posed a threat to Greek lands. The Persian Empire stretched from the Aegean Sea all the way to India, an area so vast it was beyond the imaginings of the mainland Greeks, used to their small city-states. Many Greeks believed that the Persians, who had conquered most of the known world, would turn an eye toward Greece. So when Aristagoras appeared in Sparta, saying that he wished to lead a revolt of the Greeks in Ionia against the Persians, Cleomenes was interested.

Aristagoras described the vast wealth of the Persian Empire and all the benefits that the Spartans would gain if they helped the Ionian Greeks win their freedom. Cleomenes asked Aristagoras how far the capital of the Persian Empire was from Ionia, to which he received the reply that it was three month's march. On hearing this, Cleomenes told Aristagoras that he must leave Sparta immediately, and that he would receive no help from the Spartans. Quite apart from the vast size of the Persian Empire and the resources that it contained, Cleomenes knew that he could never risk taking the Spartan army so far from home. Aristagoras left Sparta and headed to Athens, to ask the Athenians if they would aid his revolt. The

A bronze sculpture of a seated boxer

Athenians, who were less cautious than the Spartans, agreed to help the Ionians. Although the revolt eventually failed, the aid the Athenians gave to Aristagoras had far-reaching consequences for all of Greece. The Persians sought to avenge this foreign interference in their empire.

The greatest limit on Cleomenes' influence was the other Spartan king, Demaratus. Demaratus had powers to rival that of Cleomenes. The two men did not see eye to eye, and on several occasions Demaratus disrupted Cleomenes' plans. Eventually Cleomenes decided to rid himself of Demaratus and devised a plan to have his rival removed from the throne. Demaratus was the son of Ariston, who had been a king of Sparta at the same time as Anaxandridas. Demaratus was the son of Ariston's third wife and was born prematurely.

As this was not long after the marriage, Ariston's immediate reaction had been that Demaratus might not be his son. Little attention was paid to this at the time, and when Ariston died in 515 BC, Demaratus succeeded him. It was only when Cleomenes decided to depose Demaratus that the story reemerged. Cleomenes made an arrangement with Leotychidas, a cousin and bitter enemy of Demaratus, who agreed to help Cleomenes depose Demaratus. In return, Cleomenes would make sure that Leotychidas would become king in Demaratus's place.

Leotychidas declared publicly and under oath that Demaratus was not the son of Ariston and thus had no right to be king. The people were unsure what to believe, so they decided to consult the oracle at Delphi. Cleomenes was prepared for this and bribed the priestess at Delphi to give the answer he wanted. When the ambassadors from Sparta arrived at Delphi and asked whether Demaratus was the son of Ariston, the priestess replied that he was not. The Spartans declared that he had no right to be king, and he became an ordinary citizen. In his place, Leotychidas became the new second king. At first Demaratus tolerated this state of affairs. But then Leotychidas began to take pleasure in

A painting of Greek war-
riors at military practice

taunting him, asking what it was like to be an ordinary citizen after having been a king. At last Demaratus could take no more; he decided to leave Sparta. He eventually reached Persia, where he presented himself to Darius, the king of Persia, who gave him shelter. Darius was a cunning man who knew that Demaratus would prove useful to him in the future.

Cleomenes' act of bribing the priestess at Delphi was soon discovered. Fearing that he might be punished, Cleomenes fled from Sparta and traveled around Greece trying to gather support. He had been a king for almost thirty years, and he had friends in many places. When news of his activity reached Sparta, the Spartans became worried that he might build an army to march against them. So they invited him to return, promising that he would not be punished. On his return, however, Cleomenes began to behave in an alarming manner, committing unprovoked acts of violence. He was placed in jail and tied down.

The fate of Cleomenes is uncertain. According to Herodotus, who recorded the history of the Spartan government, Cleomenes demanded that his jailer give him a knife. The jailer, a helot, was so used to obeying Spartans that he provided the knife as ordered. Cleomenes began to mutilate himself, and before anyone could stop him, Cleomenes bled to death. Other historians, however, believe this was not the case. Some argue that Cleomenes was murdered by his enemies. The fact that Cleomenes had bribed the priestess at Delphi would have upset many people. The Spartans were a religious people and did not take kindly to the abuse of their religion. If Cleomenes was murdered, one man above all had ample motive: Leonidas. Cleomenes had driven Leonidas's brother Dorieus into exile. Leonidas stood to gain the throne upon Cleomenes' death. Although we don't know what really happened in that Spartan jail in 490 BC, the result was that Leonidas, the eldest surviving son of Anaxandridas, became king.

Despite the length of his reign, Cleomenes had not fathered a son. His only child was

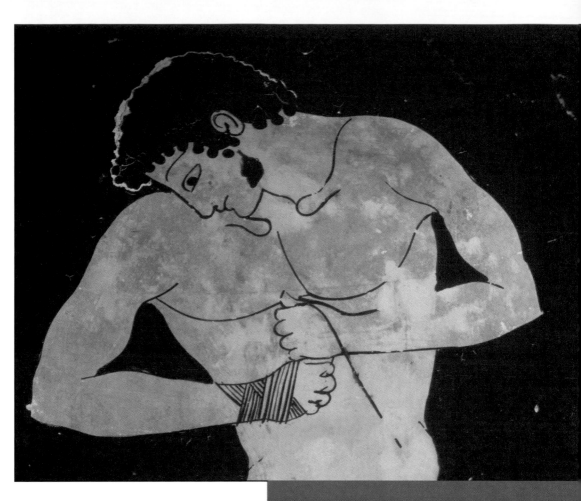

A young man binding his wrist with a leather strap prior to a wrestling match

a daughter named Gorgo. In most of Greece, women were second-class citizens. They were not considered capable of rational behavior and were treated like children. They had no political rights, were not allowed to own property, and spent most of their lives quite separate from the men. In Sparta, however, women enjoyed much more freedom. Although they did not possess the political rights of the men, women could own property and were independent in a way unknown in the rest of Greece. While foreigners often condemned the freedom the Spartans gave their women, they still showed them a grudging admiration as the most capable women in all Greece.

Gorgo was a typical Spartan woman and was famed for her wisdom and virtue. When she was still a child, and Aristagoras was visiting Cleomenes to bribe the Spartan into helping his revolt, the nine-year-old Gorgo spoke up: "You must send the stranger away, father. Otherwise he will corrupt you!" Gorgo's concern over the corrupting influence of wealth was a typical Spartan virtue. Indeed, she found the behavior of Aristagoras rather odd. Once she saw Aristagoras's servant dressing him, and remarked: "Look father, the stranger has no hands!" In most Greek cities, a wealthy man like Aristagoras would have had servants to help him do all the simple daily tasks. To a Spartan, however, brought up with a self-reliant attitude, the idea that a man would have a servant to help him dress seemed ridiculous. To the young Gorgo, the only possible explanation was that he couldn't dress himself because he had no hands.

At some point in the late 490s BC, Leonidas and Gorgo were married. The practice of an uncle marrying his niece was not uncommon in ancient Greece. However, we do not know if Leonidas and Gorgo were married before or after Cleomenes died. If Cleomenes was still alive, it is possible that he was seeking to heal the rift with Leonidas. These rivalries had been tearing the families apart for fifty years and were damaging Sparta as a whole. For his part, Leonidas knew that marrying Gorgo would further strengthen his claim to the throne.

A bronze incense burner from Delphi

On the other hand, if the marriage took place after Cleomenes' death, then it is quite possible that Cleomenes still bore a strong dislike for the younger brother of Dorieus, and would have forbidden such a marriage. Gorgo would have been about twenty when her father died, the age at which Spartan women would be expected to marry. Indeed, if Leonidas was involved in Cleomenes' death, then perhaps his motives were personal rather than political. However, all this is only speculation. We don't know whether Leonidas and Gorgo were in love, if they married against her father's will, or if Cleomenes had forbidden such a marriage. However, we do know that they soon produced an heir, Pleistarchus, who would one day be king. But Leonidas would not enjoy watching his son grow into a man. While Pleistarchus was still a child, the moment of truth for Leonidas and all Greece came upon them.

THE HERO

In 480 BC the Greek city-states faced the greatest peril in their history. The mighty Persian Empire was on the move. Xerxes, the new king of Persia, had amassed an army of enormous size. To the Greeks, it appeared as if he had brought all of Asia with him.

In the space of fifty years, the Persians had risen from being a subject people in the Median Empire to become the rulers of much of Asia. During this time, the Persians conquered Babylon, Syria, Palestine, Egypt, and Asia Minor, and even extended their influence around the Black Sea. By the beginning of the fifth century BC, Persia was the undisputed superpower of the known world. Indeed, even the Greeks referred to the Persian king as the Great King, so great was Xerxes' influence beyond his own borders.

Xerxes had good reason to invade Greece. Ten years earlier, the Athenians and their allies defeated Darius, Xerxes' father, at the Battle of Marathon. Darius wanted to punish the Athenians for helping the revolt led by Aristagoras in Ionia. He sent a force to capture Athens, and when this failed, Darius became obsessed with punishing Athens. He died before he could achieve this, so it was up Xerxes to fulfill his father's dying wish— to subdue the Greeks and destroy Athens.

For five years, Xerxes built up an army capable of invading Greece. He sent messengers throughout his vast empire and drafted men from forty-six different nations: Persians, Medes, Babylonians, Egyptians, Ethiopians, Indians, Scythians, Ionian Greeks, and many others. In later years, the Greeks would exaggerate the size of the Persian army. Herodotus recounted that the entire force, including infantry and noncombatants, numbered five million men and more than 1,000 ships. Modern historians estimate a much lower figure, about 200,000 men. To the citizens of the Greek city-states, who could muster only a few thousand men each, the Persian army was vast beyond anything they had ever experienced.

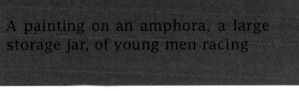

A painting on an amphora, a large storage jar, of young men racing

Xerxes also gathered around him a great number of Greek exiles, men who had been forced to leave their cities. Xerxes knew that these men would be useful during his invasion and could advise him about the Greek army. For their part, the exiles hoped that once Xerxes was successful, they might be made rulers of Greece. Among these men was Demaratus, the former king of Sparta who had been deposed by Cleomenes. When Demaratus discovered that Xerxes was preparing to march against Greece, he decided to send a message to Sparta to warn his former people. The reason he did this is uncertain; he may have wanted to taunt them with the news that they were soon to be destroyed as an act of vengeance for exiling him. Or perhaps, at heart, he remembered he was a Spartan. Whatever the case, Demaratus knew that any messenger he sent to Greece would be stopped and searched. The Greeks normally sent letters written on papyrus, a form of paper, or on wooden tablets covered with wax. These could be easily discovered, so he decided to write a message on a wooden tablet and then place wax over it, so that if inspected, it would appear to be a blank writing tablet. Even the messenger was unaware of what he carried. In this way, Demaratus managed to get the tablet to Sparta. However, once there no one could discover its purpose, until Gorgo guessed that the message was underneath the wax. Thus the Spartans became the first people in Greece to learn of Xerxes' plans.

Xerxes sent ambassadors to the Greek states to demand their submission once his preparations for the invasion were complete. Some cities refused, but many surrendered. The only cities to which he did not send ambassadors were Athens and Sparta. When Darius had sent ambassadors to these two cities ten years before, they had met with a harsh fate. In Athens, the ambassadors were thrown into the pit reserved for condemned criminals, and in Sparta, they were thrown down a well. This was not only a great insult to the Persians, but it also broke the sacred rule that all ambassadors must be well treated. While the Persians and the Athenians were already enemies, the Spartans became the Persians' enemies by this act. It happened just after Leonidas became king.

The Greek citizens were not slow to react to the news. A council was called of all the states willing to defy Xerxes; they met at Corinth in central Greece. Of the many Greek city-states, only thirty-one attended the conference. Principal among these were Sparta and Athens. Sparta was famed for her elite army, undisputedly the best in Greece, while Athens had the largest fleet and held the honor of having defeated the Persians at Marathon. The delegates at the conference quickly realized that the key to any successful defense of Greece lay in unity. The history of Greece, both ancient and modern, is one of division and infighting. But the delegates knew that against the overwhelming

A bust of Themistocles, the Athenian leader and naval commander who worked hard to keep the Greek alliance against the Persians from collapsing

power of Persia, they could only save themselves if they worked together. The Athenian leader Themistocles had conceded leadership of the Greek alliance to Sparta. This act of generosity and foresight was essential to the survival of Greece. With no disputes between the allies over the question of leadership, the alliance might, just might, succeed.

The delegates had to decide how to defend Greece. The combination of Spartan land power and Athenian naval power would have to work in unison. Initially, they decided to send a force to Tempe in northern Greece, but when the force arrived they discovered that the position was indefensible. So the council had to choose a second position. The obvious choice was the pass of Thermopylae, a narrow road between the mountains and the sea where the Persians would be likely to strike, but where the narrowness of the pass would prevent them from making use of their superiority in manpower. While the land forces held the Persian army at Thermopylae, the fleet would engage the Persians at Artemisium, just off the coast. If the Greek forces could hold the enemy at these positions, then the Persians would find it difficult to supply rations to their vast army. Moreover, the many Greek cities that had remained neutral would join the alliance once they saw that the Persians could be resisted. So the strategy was decided—Thermopylae was the gateway to Greece, as well as the bottleneck where an invading force could be stopped.

The citizens of Sparta, like all the other citizens of the Greek city-states, sent ambassadors to Delphi to consult the gods as to the outcome of the war. According to legend, the prophecy, which was delivered in verse, was a worrying one:

> Listen, O Spartans of the open plains:
> Either Xerxes will sack your gracious town,
> And place your women and children
> in chains,
> Or you will mourn a king of great renown.

The Temple of Apollo at Delphi. The Spartans sent ambassadors to Delphi to learn from the oracle if they would be successful against the Persian forces.

The mountainous terrain of central Greece shows the difficulties faced by Xerxes' army and how a small number of defenders might hold up superior forces at one of the narrow passes.

The meaning of the prophecy was clear: Either a Spartan king would die, or the city itself would be destroyed. Once the news of the prophecy reached Sparta, Leonidas decided to take only 300 Spartans with him, accompanied by about 700 helots. Leonidas called for volunteers. He would take only those soldiers who had sons, so that no family line would die out. He is also said to have celebrated his own funeral, the usual honor for a dead hero, before he left Sparta, thus showing his certainty that he would not return. He bid farewell to his wife Gorgo. She asked him if he had any last instructions for her, to which he replied, "Marry a good man, and have good children."

Modern historians reject the story that Leonidas went to Thermopylae expecting to die. They account for the small size of the Spartan force on the grounds that most Spartans did not want to send their troops so far north. For the Spartans, the natural defensive position was at the Isthmus of Corinth, the thin stretch of land that linked the Peloponnese to the rest of mainland Greece. This position, they believed, could be easily defended against the vast Persian army. The only reason to send troops farther north would be to protect the Greek cities, such as Athens, that were located in that part of Greece. Why should the Spartans waste men and resources defending someone else?

However, there were some people in Sparta who did not think this way. While it was true that the Spartans and other Peloponnesian cities could defend the Isthmus at Corinth without the protection of the Athenian fleet, the Persian navy could land troops anywhere on the coast of the Peloponnese. If the Spartans showed that they were not willing to send troops north of the isthmus, then the alliance would collapse. The citizens of those cities north of the isthmus, Athens among them, would realize that they could not resist the Persians alone and would be forced to surrender. The only force that could oppose the Persian navy was the fleet of Athens. If Athens was lost, then so was all of Greece. In effect, defending cities such as Athens was a matter of self-interest for the Spartans because without Athens, Sparta was doomed.

Leonidas was one of the few who realized this. When he marched north to Thermopylae, it may well have been without the full support of the Spartan government. Moreover, there was a religious festival taking place at the time, and it was against tradition to send out an army during this festival. For the Spartan government, the festival provided a useful excuse for not sending the full army to Thermopylae.

The fact that Leonidas took only 300 men with him is significant. The royal bodyguard, which the king personally commanded, numbered 300. Leonidas was leading his personal bodyguard to defend Greece, while the Spartan government hesitated. He knew that if the Spartan army was seen to march, then other city-states would send troops, and the alliance might survive. If Leonidas could hold the pass of Thermopylae long enough, then even the Spartans would have to act.

At first Leonidas was proven right. As he marched north, he gathered troops from the cities he passed. Tegea, a long-standing ally of Sparta, and the towns of the Arcadia region added more than 1,500 troops. Mantinea added another 500, Corinth 400, and little Mycenae, the city that in legend had, 800 years before, led all Greece against Troy, added 80 men. Locris and Phocis, in whose territory Thermopylae lay, added more than 1,000 men between them. The city of Thespiae sent almost their entire fighting strength, 700 men, who would become legends in their own right. Thebes, the greatest city of central Greece, sent 400 men. When Leonidas reached Thermopylae, he had nearly 7,000 men under his command. Surely this would be enough to hold the

This painting shows Greek infantry putting on their armor.

narrow pass until the rest of Greece was spurred into action by their example.

Meanwhile, Xerxes' army was on the march. When he reached the Hellespont (also known as the Dardanelle Straits), the small channel that separates Europe from Asia, he built a bridge so that his army could march across the sea. When Xerxes reached the peninsula of Mount Athos in northern Greece, his men dug a canal through it so that his fleet would not have to sail around the peninsula. It was as if he controlled nature itself—Xerxes' army had marched across the sea and his navy had sailed across the land. Rumors quickly spread about the size of the army. It was said that when Xerxes' army marched, it took seven days to pass; when they set up camp there were so many men that they drank the rivers dry. Each city the Persians reached submitted to Xerxes and attempted to play host to him.

Indeed, many cities were financially ruined trying to entertain Xerxes and his army for a single night.

While on the march, Xerxes sent for Demaratus, who was accompanying the army. Xerxes asked Demaratus whether the Greeks would attempt to resist his army. "Surely," claimed Xerxes, "all the peoples of the west united could not stand against me." Demaratus replied that valor was the way of the Greeks. He said of the Spartans, "Firstly, they will never submit to you on any terms that mean slavery; and secondly, they will resist you even if the rest of Greece does not. And do not ask if they have enough men. If only a thousand of them take the field, then they will fight!" Xerxes laughed at this and dismissed the idea as nonsense. "If the Greeks are free to do as they please," he said, "then it is inconceivable that they should choose to fight. If, like my Persians, they were subject to one master, then perhaps . . . But free men? Never!" Demaratus tried to explain: "Yes, the Greeks are free, but they have one master, the law. This they obey. And its command never varies, to stand firm whatever the odds, to conquer or to die."

Soon Xerxes' army reached the plain of Malis. Just ahead of the Persian army lay the

A vase painting that shows Persian and Greek warriors in hand-to-hand combat.

twin peaks of Mounts Oeta and Callidromos, sheer walls of rock that guarded the passage to Greece. The only road along the coast passed through the narrows at Thermopylae. Local informants quickly told Xerxes that the pass was already held by a Greek force under the command of a Spartan king. As the mighty army made camp, Xerxes dispatched a scout to discover if this was true, and if the Greeks were really preparing to resist him.

The lone horseman approached Thermopylae warily, and remaining beyond bow-shot, studied the Greek positions. Much of the Greek army was camped behind a wall in the center of the pass, but a few hundred men could be seen in front of it. The scout noticed that these men were doing the strangest things. Some stood guard in bright breastplates that glinted in the sun, wearing flowing red cloaks. Others were semi-naked and were practicing exercise routines. Others merely sat nearby, carefully combing their hair into long braids. None of these men took any notice of the scout, and having noted all that he saw, he returned to Xerxes and gave the king a full report.

Not understanding what the scout described, Xerxes called Demaratus and asked him to explain this strange behavior. "When you asked me before," began Demaratus, "you did not believe my answer. Well, now they are here. These men your scout describes are the Spartans, my own people, and they are preparing to resist you. It is the Spartan custom that when we are about to risk our lives, we pay careful attention to our hair. Death comes but once, and it is only right that we should be suitably attired. These are the best soldiers in all Greece. If you can defeat them, and those Spartans still at home, then Greece will be yours."

But even as he heard these words, Xerxes turned and viewed the vast number of troops at his command. This was the army that had conquered all of Asia. The few thousand Greeks in the pass could not resist the inevitable. The mere sight of this horde would surely humble them into submission, just as the Greeks of Thessaly and Macedonia had submitted. So Xerxes waited. Soon, he prophesied, the Greek resolve would crumble.

Leonidas had arrived at the pass of Thermopylae in the middle of August in 480 BC. Immediately he set about improving the position to resist the enemy. In the middle of the pass, where it was narrowest, lay the remains of a wall that the Phocians had built a century before. Leonidas rebuilt the wall as a strong fortification

Hoplites going into battle

across the pass. However, the Greeks would not fight behind it. The wall would be a shelter for the Greek camp, a place for the reserves and wounded to wait out the battle. The heavily armored Greek infantry, the *hoplites*, would fight in the open, man against man, as the Greeks had always fought.

Soon after Leonidas and his army arrived, problems began to arise. The shepherds who lived on the mountain saw the Greek army, and some of them came down to greet Leonidas. They brought worrying news. The pass at Thermopylae was not the only way through the mountains. There was another path, known as

the Anopaea, which bypassed Thermopylae completely. Starting on the plain of Malis, this path headed through the mountains, emerging at the village of Alpenoi behind the Spartan positions. Leonidas acted quickly. He dispatched the Phocian contingent, some 1,000 men, to guard the Anopaea path. This path was even narrower than the pass at Thermopylae, and if 6,000 could hold Thermopylae, then 1,000 should be able to hold Anopaea. Moreover, the Phocians were local people. They would be guarding their homes and would fight all the more fiercely. Some modern historians have suggested that Leonidas should have put a Spartan in charge of the Phocians, or reinforced their ranks with 100 of his own men. But Leonidas knew that this was impossible. The Phocians, like all Greeks, were proudly independent and would not take kindly to the hint that they were incapable of defending their own country. Within the fragile alliance, Leonidas could not afford to upset his allies. Moreover, Leonidas needed his few Spartans to fight at Thermopylae.

Leonidas's problems began to multiply a few days later. At first, all the Greeks saw was a dust cloud on the horizon. Then the scouts returned with the news. The Persians were coming. As the hours passed, the enemy forces began to spread onto the plain of Malis like floodwaters seeping across the land. Soon the entire plain was a seething mass of humanity, and still they kept coming. As Xerxes had hoped, the sight of this army sent a shiver through the Greeks. The commanders of the allied contingents started to raise their doubts. Retreat, they said, is the only option. To stand there was futile. But Leonidas would have none of it. He knew full well that if the Greek army retreated at the first sight of the Persians, then the war was lost. Many of the cities that had not already submitted to the Persians were considering surrender. Now they were waiting to see what would happen at

Thermopylae. If the alliance was to survive, then the Greeks had to fight. Retreat now would mean conquest and slavery.

While Leonidas urged his allies to stand firm, the 300 Spartans needed no such encouragement. This was what they were born for. Since the age of seven they had trained for the ultimate contest, and now it lay before them. The best soldiers in all of Greece were about to test their skill against the greatest army the world had ever seen. Many refugees passed through the Greek camp, fleeing south from the Persians. They brought with them tales of the grandeur of Xerxes and the unimaginable size of his army. One of these travelers, seeking to impress the soldiers with what he had seen, warned them sternly, "The Persians are so many that when they fire their bows their arrows block out the sun itself!" This dark image passed through the minds of the soldiers, filling them with dread at the size of Xerxes' invading forces. The Spartans alone were unperturbed. A warrior named Dieneces turned to face the soldiers who sat huddled in the pass, and with a wry smile he announced, "This is good news this stranger brings us. If the arrows of the Persians block out the sun, then we will have our battle in the shade!"

For four days Xerxes waited, hoping that the nerve of the Greeks would break. During this time, we are told, he sent ambassadors to speak to Leonidas. Xerxes was no fool, and knew, just as Leonidas knew, that if the Greeks surrendered here, then all of Greece would fall. At first, Xerxes tried to buy Leonidas's favor. If a former Spartan king such as Demaratus would join him, then perhaps the present Spartan king could also be bought. Thus, the first messenger offered Leonidas power: Join with Xerxes, and he will make you ruler of all Greece. Leonidas replied in front of his men, "Tell Xerxes this. The Greeks await his boasted army. And tell him that if he understood what is honorable in life, then he would no longer try taking things that belong to others. And tell him that for me to die for my people is a far greater honor than he can ever offer."

The messenger returned with this rejection, so Xerxes sent another ambassador with a second message. "Xerxes wishes the Greeks to be his friends, and if they give up their arms, he will allow them to return to their homes with better lands than those they now possess." Again Leonidas replied in the presence of his men, "If the Great King wishes us as allies, then we can serve him better with our arms; and if we are to resist him, then we will also need them. And as to the lands he offers us, tell him that the Greeks have long learned to win new lands by courage, not by cowardice." By this time Xerxes was furious. How dare this Greek respond to him in this way. Another messenger was sent with a final offer. "Xerxes the Great King orders the Greeks to give up their arms." Leonidas's response was short and to the point. "Come and take them!"

At last Xerxes' patience had reached its limit. The first ranks of the Persian army sprang into action. Xerxes sent down the order for the Greeks to be brought before him in chains. He would soon punish their insolence. The Medes, a proud warrior people who had once ruled much of Asia, led the first attack. Alongside the Medes, Xerxes placed the descendants of those who had fallen at Marathon ten years before, men who had great reason to hate the Greeks. As the enemy approached, the Greeks drew up their front line—a solid wall of bronze shields. A Greek scout ran back to the front line, declaring that the Persians were almost upon them. A smile crossed Leonidas's face. "Then *we* are almost upon *them*!"

A vase painting of a running Greek hoplite, or foot soldier, with shield, helmet, and spear

The Medes came in waves against the Greek shields, but each wave broke on the solid wall of bronze. Soon it was obvious that the light Persian armor was no match for the heavy armor of the Greek hoplites, and the Medes fell fast. But the Medes were no cowards and continued in the attack, trampling the bodies of the wounded and dying beneath their feet. According to Herodotus, Xerxes watched the battle from a hill that overlooked the pass. It occurred to him that even though he had many men in his army, he had few *soldiers*.

The battle continued throughout the day, and at last the Medes withdrew, battered and beaten. Xerxes then ordered the 10,000 men of his elite bodyguard into the attack. They were known as the Immortals, because whenever one of them fell, he was instantly replaced so that they were always at full strength. These men, the

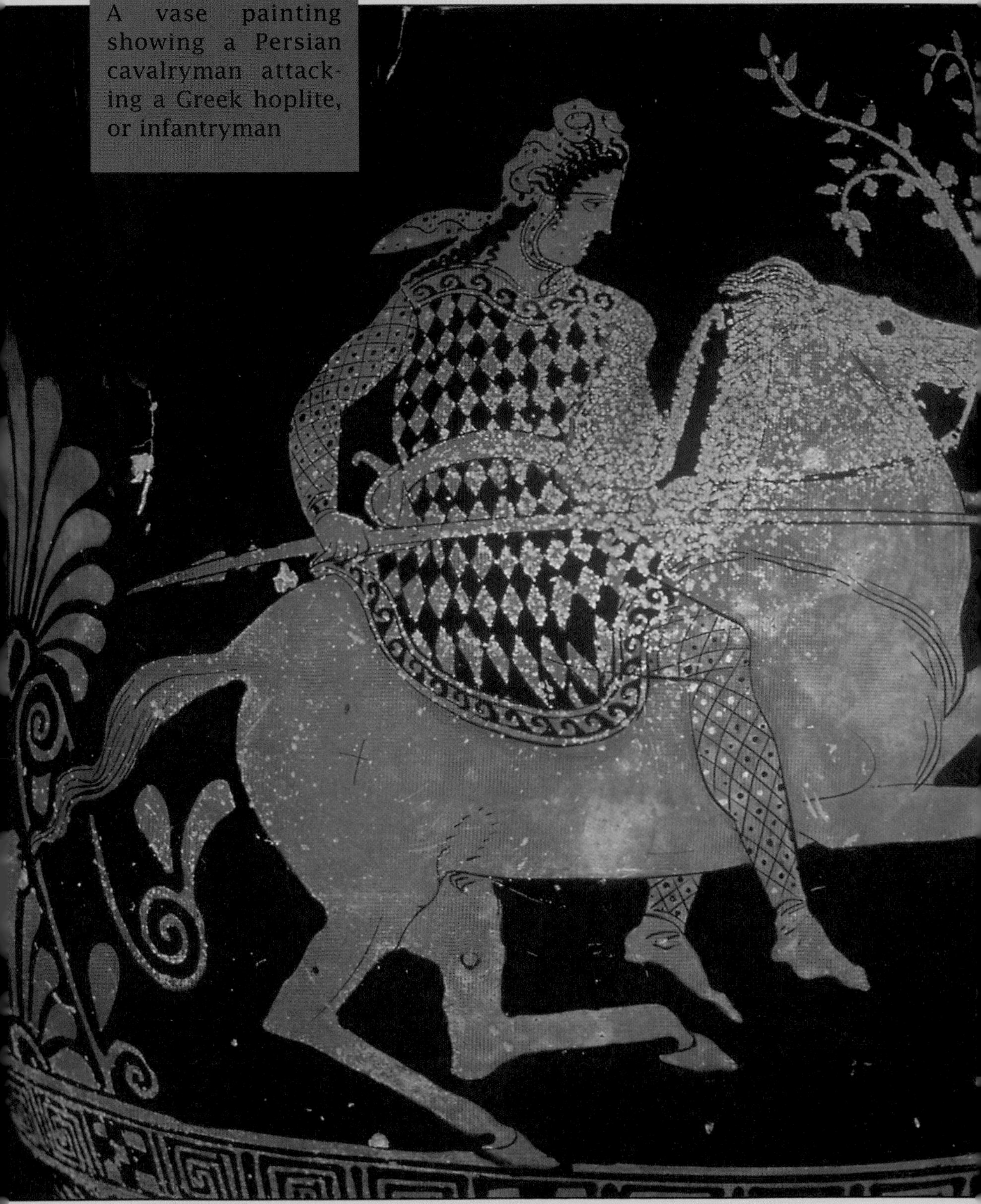

A vase painting showing a Persian cavalryman attacking a Greek hoplite, or infantryman

pride of Persia, marched forward proudly. They were dressed in long tunics embroidered with the most beautiful designs, and they wore breastplates composed of metal pieces fashioned like the scales of a fish. Yet once again, their light wicker shields and short spears could make no impression upon the Greek line. In the narrows of the pass, the Immortals could not bring their superior numbers to bear.

During the attack, the Spartans fought with a cool professionalism. At a given signal, the Spartan line broke and fell back as if in a panicked retreat. The Persians, sensing victory, gave chase, breaking their own formation. Then, at a second signal, the Spartan line suddenly reformed and pushed through the broken Persian ranks, cutting them savagely to the ground. The superior skills of the Spartan warriors and their years of training showed as they made short work of the Persian elite. Legend has it that Xerxes, watching the slaughter of his bodyguard, leapt three times to his feet in horror. Against all reason, these Greek madmen were actually resisting him.

As the sun set, the Persian forces withdrew, having learned in the hardest possible way the value of superior training and equipment. Xerxes still had the advantage, however, and where one unit had failed to defeat the Greeks, a dozen others waited anxiously to impress their king. On the next day, the attack continued. The Persians hoped that the Greeks would eventually be worn down by the unending assaults. However, Leonidas had organized his army into units according to their city, so that each man fought next to his countrymen, and each unit was replaced before it could tire. Thus, the second day passed, and the Persians were driven back again.

All this time, Xerxes and his officers wondered if there was another way through the mountains. They knew that all mountain ranges contained numerous footpaths and goat tracks. However, was there a path that an army could follow? Scouts had been exploring the mountains, but as yet they had found nothing. They needed a guide—someone prepared to lead the army safely across the cliffs and ravines. On the evening of the second day of the battle, Ephialtes, a local shepherd, was brought into the presence of the Persian king. He quickly told Xerxes of the path at Anopaea, and for a price, he was willing to guide the Persians over the mountain. In return for gold, he would betray his fellow Greeks who, even as he spoke, were recovering from two days of hard battle in the pass.

As darkness fell, the Immortals, led by General Hydarnes and guided by Ephialtes, set out from the Persian camp. The initial desperation caused by their defeat the previous day quickly evaporated, and the Immortals sensed that they would now exact revenge on the Greeks. They marched steadily through the night, through the thick oak forests that covered the mountain. At the first signs of dawn, the Immortals approached the summit. After marching for eight hours, they were glad to reach a place to rest. But as they emerged from the forest into the meadows on the mountain's summit, they were shocked to see Greek soldiers preparing for battle. Suddenly worried, Hydarnes turned to Ephialtes and asked him, who are these men? Are they the Spartans? Ephialtes calmed his fears. No, these men were the Phocians, local men, and nothing like the Spartans. Hydarnes, relieved at this news, drew up his men for battle.

Although Leonidas had ordered the Phocians to guard the Anopaea several days before, they had not expected the enemy to appear. The first they heard of the enemy's presence was the rustling of fallen leaves; they immediately prepared to resist them. However, the Phocians were not experienced soldiers like the Spartans. As the Persians began to rain arrows down on the Greek troops, they retreated to the summit of the mountain. Forming a wall of shields, they prepared to fight the Persians to the last man.

Hydarnes noticed the Phocians' maneuver with satisfaction—they had made a fatal mistake. Assuming that they were the main focus of the attack, the Phocians withdrew from their position; they were no longer blocking the Anopaea. Hydarnes drew up a line of archers to keep the Phocians pinned down on the summit, then marched the main body of his force past them and down the mountain. Even as the Phocians stood beneath the hail of Persian arrows, helplessly watching the Immortals pass by, they must have thought that they had failed Leonidas. Thermopylae would fall.

Back at Thermopylae, the Spartans received a glimpse of the coming catastrophe.

Deserters from the Persian army, including Ionian Greeks who had been conscripted into Xerxes' legions, were now crossing over into the Spartan positions. One of them, a man named Tyrrehastiades from the city of Cyme, told Leonidas of the departure of the Immortals and the presence of a traitor who was guiding them. Finally, scouts posted in the mountains returned with the news. The Phocians had failed.

A wave of fear swept the Greek camp, and Leonidas called a meeting of all the commanders. The determination they had shown in two days of battle was fast disappearing. To stay was to die. Of that there was no doubt. But retreat would be disastrous. If the Greek army retreated at the first setback, then what hope would there be for the alliance? If Sparta fled from the Persians, then no one else would resist. The other Greek city-states would have proof of what they already suspected, that Sparta was not committed to the alliance. Moreover, they would conclude that Xerxes was invincible. The only hope the alliance had of holding together was Sparta's commitment to the war effort, and some evidence that, despite the odds, Xerxes could be resisted. Then, perhaps, the Athenians and their

A group of running Greek hoplites. This painting illustrates how the Greek infantry phalanx could form a wall of bronze shields against the enemy, each man partially protecting the man next to him.

fleet, so necessary to the hopes of Greece, would continue to resist. And perhaps all those city-states wavering between resistance and surrender would choose to fight.

Yet at the same time, Leonidas realized, these brave allies who had fought so well did not need to perish. These were good soldiers who now had experience fighting the Persians, and who now understood how to take advantage of the superiority of the Greek equipment. They would be indispensable in the battles that were to come. Moreover, they could take the message to their respective cities and to every Greek with courage who wished to be free—the Persians *can* be resisted.

So Leonidas sent out the orders: The allies were to retreat; the Spartans would stay. But even as this order was given, some voices went up in protest. The Thespians volunteered to stay. Brave amateurs, they had not, like the Spartans, prepared their entire lives for a moment such as this. While every Spartan was a soldier first and foremost, the Thespians were farmers and carpenters, workmen and craftsmen, who had taken up their weapons when their city was threatened. They volunteered, making this last stand a Greek, not just a Spartan, act. The Thebans also volunteered to stay, knowing that the majority of the Thebans at home had chosen to surrender. By staying with Leonidas, perhaps they could erase some of the shame of their fellow citizens. Alongside them, the tiny contingent from Mycenae also volunteered to stay, determined that they too should partake in the glory. The men of Thespiae, Thebes, and Mycenae, who could have retreated and lived, instead chose to remain and die. They chose the Spartan way. Although not a Spartan, the priest Megistias refused to desert his king. After all, Leonidas needed the help of the gods in this, his last and greatest venture.

As the sun rose over Thermopylae, the main body of the Greek army marched toward the south, watched by the Spartans, Thespians, and Thebans. Leonidas passed the word around to those who remained. They should eat their breakfast in the expectation that their next meal would be in Hades, in the underworld.

Various stories recall the last day at Thermopylae. Some traditional tales describe a final Greek attack on the Persian camp itself. Knowing he could no longer hold the pass, Leonidas decided to lead his men in a surprise assault, descending upon the Persian camp and creating havoc. It is said that the Greeks even reached Xerxes' tent and would have killed the Persian king had he not fled into the night. Once the Persians realized just how few Greeks had attacked them, the Persians launched a counterattack, defeating the Greeks after a savage battle. However thrilling this story is, many historians believe it to have been invented long after the event.

Herodotus, who spoke to some of Xerxes' soldiers long after the battle, recounts a different story. According to Herodotus, before Hydarnes and the Immortals left Thermopylae for Anopaea, the two men set a plan in motion. Xerxes had arranged with Hydarnes that he would attack the Greeks in the middle of the morning, thus giving the Immortals enough time to descend the mountain and attack Leonidas and his troops from the rear. At this time the Persians drew up their lines and prepared to attack. For the first two days of the battle at Thermopylae, the Greeks had fought at the narrowest point of the pass so that the Persians could not make use of their superior numbers. However, knowing that this was to be their last battle, Leonidas led his men out of the narrows of the pass. On a wider front, the Greeks could inflict greater casualties upon their enemy.

The battle that followed was savage beyond belief. Knowing that the end was near, the Greeks fought ferociously. Herodotus describes the carnage of trampled bodies and men who were forced into the sea and drowned. The Persian officers used whips on their own men to keep them fighting the Greeks with equal ferocity. In the slaughter, many Persians were killed, including two of Xerxes' brothers.

At some point during the battle, Leonidas was killed. The fighting focused around his body as the Persians tried to drag it away and the Greeks tried to retrieve it. Eventually, the Greeks recovered the body of the Spartan king. Soon after, word spread through the surviving Greeks that the Immortals had arrived and were advancing on their rear. The Greeks retreated into the narrows of the pass, taking the body of Leonidas with them. Still they resisted, some with spears and swords,

A detail of a warrior with a spear from a sixth-century-BC vase painting

others with their bare fists and teeth. They reached a small hill that stands at the very center of the pass, and there they formed a tight shield wall. Soon they were completely surrounded, but the Persians, still afraid of the frenzy that had taken hold of the Greeks, kept their distance. At the signal, the Persians drew their bows and showered arrows upon the Greeks. The remaining Greeks held their shields aloft, but volley after volley of Persian arrows fell upon them. One by one the Greeks went down, arrows piercing the gaps in their armor and the increasing gaps in the wall of shields. The volleys continued until the last Greek fell.

A mighty cry went up from the Persians, who rushed forward with their blades drawn, to ensure that all the Greeks were dead. Xerxes stood by somberly watching the scene, for he felt little satisfaction in this victory. Leonidas's body was brought before Xerxes and beheaded. Leonidas's head—the head of the man who had resisted Xerxes—was stuck on a pole and displayed for all to see. This is the fate, he declared, of those who resist Xerxes, the Great King.

Xerxes, king of all Asia, and his Persian army marched south, past the massed bodies of Greeks and Persians in the pass, past the circle of corpses upon the hill, past the bloody head of Leonidas. They marched on through Thermopylae. The gateway to Greece was open.

EPILOGUE: THE LEGEND

King Xerxes and his army marched through Greece, unstoppable. Those who had already submitted to Persia were spared, but those who had dared to join the alliance were destroyed. Phocis, Thespiae, and Plataea were pillaged and sacked. The population of Athens fled the city to the island of Salamis just off the coast. From there the Athenians witnessed the flames as the Persians destroyed their homes and slaughtered the few who had remained behind.

Morale was low after the defeat at Thermopylae. The Greek fleet, which had engaged the Persians at Artemisium, retreated to Salamis. The alliance itself seemed on the verge of collapse as the Spartans began to fortify the Isthmus of Corinth. Had Leonidas retreated from Thermopylae on the last day of the battle or submitted to

Xerxes, then the Spartan government may well have remained in the good graces of the Persians. But because Leonidas and his troops stood up to the invaders, the Spartan officials were shamed into action; they saw it as their duty to avenge the death of their king.

Themistocles, the Athenian king, succeeded in convincing Spartan admiral Eurybiades to fight at Salamis. Themistocles knew that the other Greeks would only remain if the Spartans did so. And so the Greek fleet sailed against the Persians in September of 480 BC. The Greek naval victory struck terror into the heart of Xerxes. The Persian king had seen enough of these battle-crazed Greeks. He left his army in the hands of his generals and returned to Persia, claiming that he was needed at home to run the empire. Xerxes had faith that his generals would finish off the Greek resistance. In the following year, the Persian army met the combined Greek forces near the city of Plataea. Before, at Thermopylae, the Persians faced only 300 Spartans and a total of 7,000 Greek allies. Now they faced 5,000 Spartans and 40,000 Greeks. During the battle, a Spartan named Aemnestus killed Persian general Mardonius, thus avenging Leonidas. The Persian line collapsed, and Greece was saved.

A view of the statue of King Leonidas at Thermopylae

Leonidas was not forgotten; statues of him were erected in Sparta. Beside a magnificent tomb dedicated to Leonidas stood a monument that listed the names of the 300 men who had died with him at Thermopylae. Yet today we know the names of only a few. There was Dieneces, the wit, and two brothers, Aplheus and Maron, who died together. Also among the fallen was Eurytus, who was blinded by illness, but still insisted on fighting. Beside their names are those of the Thespians and Thebans, which Herodotus records: the Thespian leader Demophilus; Dithyrambus, remembered as the bravest of the Thespians; and the Thebans Anaxander and Leontiades.

Among all those who died, it was Leonidas who became a legend. For hundreds of years after his death, athletic contests were held every year in his honor. Poets wrote verses recounting Leonidas's glory, which the Spartans sang at holy festivals. And as time passed, so the legend grew. Leonidas became not just the hero of Thermopylae but the ideal hero—brave and honest, always true to his word, and unflinching in battle. His sacrifice was not just a military act but a moral one. When faced with the choice to live or die, Leonidas chose to die a free man.

This image of Leonidas as the perfect hero has survived for 2,500 years. Poets of the Middle Ages saw Leonidas as the perfect knight. In the late eighteenth century French revolutionaries hailed the Spartan king as a democratic hero. Monarchists have seen him as the ideal king, dedicated to his people. And republicans have praised him as a man of the people who died alongside his men. Hundreds of books, plays, and poems have been written about him. He is the subject of many paintings and, more recently, films. A modern statue of Leonidas, in full armor and brandishing his sword, stands in Sparta today. At Thermopylae, there stands another modern statue, in which Leonidas defiantly waves his spear.

Yet the most suitable monument to Leonidas is an inscription upon a stone that sits on the hill where the last of the Greeks died. A modern stone has replaced the ancient stone, but the inscription is the same. It is a simple poem, written soon after the battle, asking the traveler who passes this place to do one last favor for the dead. It does not boast about what the Spartans had done. Like the Spartans, it is simple, straightforward, and honest:

> Go and tell the Spartans, passer by,
> That here, as they would expect, we lie.

GLOSSARY

Anaxander The commander of the Theban contingent at Thermopylae.

Anaxandridas A king of Sparta, reigned c. 560–520 BC; father of Cleomenes, Dorieus, Leonidas, and Cleombrotus.

Anopaea The path through the mountains south of Thermopylae, by which the pass at Thermopylae could be outflanked.

Ariston A king of Sparta, reigned c. 550–515 BC; father of Demaratus.

Cleombrotus The youngest son of Anaxandridas, brother of Dorieus and Leonidas, and half-brother of Cleomenes; briefly commanded Spartan forces after Thermopylae, but died soon after in 480 BC.

Cleomenes A king of Sparta, reigned c. 520–490 BC; half-brother of Dorieus, Leonidas, and Cleombrotus, father of Gorgo; died in 490 BC.

colonies From the tenth to the seventh centuries BC, it was common practice for a polis to send out settlers to found a new city. The new city would become a "colony" of the mother city. This was not a colony in the modern sense; although the colony would retain close ties with its mother city, it was an independent state. By founding colonies, the Greeks spread their influence throughout the Mediterranean.

Darius A king of Persia, reigned 521–486 BC; invaded Greece in 490 BC, but was defeated by a combined force of Athenians and Plataeans at Marathon; father of Xerxes.

Delphi Located in central Greece; the site of one of the most important religious centers in the ancient world. Greeks traveled from all over the Mediterranean to consult the god Apollo or to ask questions of the priestess or oracle, called the Pythia, expecting her to prophesize the course of future events. Pythia's prophesies were often in the form of a poem; her words were interpreted by a male prophet.

Demaratus A king of Sparta, reigned c. 515–491 BC; deposed by Cleomenes; accompanied Xerxes on his invasion of Greece. After the war, Demaratus retired to Asia Minor, on lands given to him by Xerxes.

Demophilus The commander of the Thespian contingent at Thermopylae.

Dorieus Elder brother of Leonidas and Cleombrotus; younger half-brother of Cleomenes; left Sparta around 515 BC and was killed in Sicily.

Ephialtes A Greek from Malis who led the Persians through the Anopaea path that outflanks the pass at

Thermopylae. After the war a price was put on his head, and he was murdered.

ephors Annually elected magistrates in Sparta.

gerousia The Spartan council of elders.

Gorgo The Daughter of Cleomenes and wife of Leonidas.

helots The slave population of Sparta.

Herodotus A historian and author of a historical account of the Greek and Persian wars. Born in the city of Halicarnassus (in modern Turkey) in about 485 BC, Herodotus is considered to be the first historian and has been called the "father of history." While some scholars have questioned the truth of some of his claims, there can be no doubt that without his work, called *History*, our knowledge of ancient Greece would be lacking.

hoplite The heavily armored infantryman who served as the backbone of the Greek armies. Each man wore a heavy breastplate and helmet and carried a large round shield made of bronze called a *hoplon*. At his side he carried a short sword, but his main weapon was a spear some nine feet long. The hoplites fought in what is known as a phalanx, a tightly packed formation of men designed to be almost impenetrable. Because the shield was always carried on the left arm, it only protected the left side of the man who carried it. A hoplite's right side was protected by the shield of the man to his right, while his own shield protected the man to his left. Thus each man was protected by someone else's shield. The phalanx could only work when each man was prepared to trust his neighboring comrade with his life. If a man dropped his shield, the first man to die would be his neighbor, and this responsibility gave men extra courage.

Immortals The elite soldiers of the Persian army and the personal bodyguard of the king.

Lycurgus A semi-mythical lawgiver of Sparta believed to have devised its unusual social and political system. He was regarded as one of the great wise men of Greece, though even the Spartans admitted that they knew virtually nothing about him. Plutarch wrote a biography about him, which is contained in Plutarch's *Lives*.

Marathon A broad plain twenty-six miles northeast of Athens; site of the famous Greek victory over the Persians in 490 BC.

Megistias A priest from Arcanania, who served with Leonidas at Thermopylae and died during the battle in 480 BC.

Phocis An area in central Greece comprised of several cities that combined to form a federal state. The Phocians joined Leonidas at Thermopylae, but failed to hold the Anopaea path, resulting in defeat.

Plutarch A historian and biographer, c. AD 50–AD 120. Considered one of the most important sources of Greek history, Plutarch wrote *Lives*, which included biographies of many leading figures from Greek and Roman history. Plutarch used a wide range of sources that are not available today.

polis The form of city-state found in ancient Greece.

Salamis An island near Athens; site of the Greek naval victory over the Persians in 480 BC.

Themistocles The Athenian king who played a major role in the defeat of the Persian invasion of 480 BC.

Thespiae A city in central Greece; Thespian soldiers volunteered to stay with Leonidas at Thermopylae to oppose the Persian invasion.

Xerxes A king of Persia, reigned c. 485 to 465 BC; son of Darius. Xerxes invaded Greece in 480 BC with a large army; assassinated in 465 BC.

FOR MORE INFORMATION

American Classical League
Miami University
Oxford, OH 45056
e-mail: info@aclclassics.org
Web site: http://www.aclclassics.org

The Classical Association
Room 323, Third Floor
Senate House
London WC1E 7HU
United Kingdom
+44 20 7862 8706
e-mail: croberts@sas.ac.uk
Web site: http://www.sas.ac.uk/icls/
  ClassAss

International Plutarch Society
Department of History
Utah State University
0710 Old Main Hill
Logan, UT 84322-0710
Web site: http://www.usu.edu/history/
  plout.htm

National Junior Classical League
Miami University
Oxford, OH 45056-1694
(513) 529-7741
Web site: http://www.njcl.org

WEB SITES

Due to the changing nature of Internet links, the Rosen Publishing Group, Inc., has developed an online list of Web sites related to the subject of this book. This site is updated regularly. Please use this link to access the list:

http://www.rosenlinks.com/lag/leon/

FOR FURTHER READING

Bradford, E. *The Year of Thermopylae.* London: Macmillan, 1980.

Cassin-Scott, J. *The Greek and Persian Wars.* London: Osprey, 1977.

Golding, W. *The Hot Gates and Other Occasional Pieces.* London: Faber, 1965.

Hanson, V. D. *The Wars of the Ancient Greeks.* London: Cassell, 1999.

Sekunda, N. *The Spartan Army.* London: Osprey, 1998.

BIBLIOGRAPHY

Burn, A.R. *Persia and the Greeks.*
London: Duckworth, 1984.

Forrest, W. G. *A History of Sparta.*
Bristol, England: Bristol Classical
Press, 1995.

Green, P. *The Greco-Persian Wars.*
Berkeley, CA: University of California
Press, 1966.

Hanson, V. D. *The Western Way of War.*
New York: Knopf, 1989.

Hignett, C. *Xerxes' Invasion of
Greece.* Oxford, England: Clarendon
Press, 1963.

Hooker, J. T. *The Ancient Spartans.*
London: J. M. Dent, 1980.

Lazenby, J. *The Defence of Greece.*
Warminster, England: Aris &
Phillips, 1993.

Lazenby, J. *The Spartan Army.*
Warminster, England: Aris &
Phillips, 1985.

Plutarch. *The Life of Lycurgus.* London:
Penguin, 1988.

Todd, S. *Athens and Sparta.* London:
Duckworth, 1996.

INDEX

ABOUT THE AUTHOR

Ian Macgregor Morris was born in 1971 to a Scottish father and Dutch mother, and spent much of his early life traveling between Britain and the Netherlands. Educated at Rugby School, he went on to earn his B.A. at University College London, and his Ph.D. at the University of Manchester. He has worked extensively on ancient and modern history, carried out archaeological fieldwork in Greece, and worked on television documentaries on Greek history. He is currently an Honorary University Fellow in the Department of Classics and Ancient History, University of Exeter.

CREDITS

EDITOR
Jake Goldberg

DESIGN
Evelyn Horovicz

LAYOUT
Hillary Arnold